A WALK THROUGH

Graceland Cemetery

A WALK THROUGH

Graceland Cemetery

by Barbara Lanctot

photographs by John Alderson,
Ned Costello, and Rosemary Kluke

A CHICAGO ARCHITECTURE FOUNDATION WALKING TOUR

Published by
Chicago Architecture Foundation
1800 S. Prairie Avenue
Chicago, Illinois 60616

First printing 1977
Revised edition 1982
Revised edition 1988
Fourth printing 1992

ISBN 0-9620562-2-7

Published through the
Marilyn Schneider Memorial Fund

Design by Rosemary Kluke

Cover photo: Getty Tomb
Frontispiece: Looking west from Lambert Tree's grave

PREFACE

The Chicago Architecture Foundation is a nonprofit organization dedicated to increasing public awareness and understanding of Chicago's past, present, and future architectural and planned environment.

The organization was founded in 1966 to save the John J. Glessner House, the only remaining structure of four that noted architect Henry Hobson Richardson designed for Chicago. The Foundation maintains Glessner House, restored to its 1890 appearance, as a historic house museum in the Prairie Avenue Historical District. The house has been declared a Chicago and national landmark.

In 1977, the City of Chicago moved its oldest structure, the Henry B. Clarke House, to the Prairie Avenue Historic District adjacent to Glessner House. Clarke House, restored to the period 1860, was opened to the public in 1982. The Clarke House Museum is operated through a collaborative effort by the Chicago Architecture Foundation, the City of Chicago, and the National Society of the Colonial Dames of America in the State of Illinois.

The Chicago Architecture Foundation also operates the ArchiCenter in the historic Monadnock Building. ArchiCenter is an exhibition gallery, lecture and tour center, and museum store devoted to the built environment. The Foundation also trains volunteer docents who give architectural bus, bike, and walking tours throughout the Chicago area.

The Graceland Cemetery tour was developed by docents in 1975, with the cooperation of cemetery manager Frank Luto. The walk, presented here in written form, does not cover all the noteworthy graves in the cemetery. It concentrates on the area surrounding the man-made lake, the area richest in beauty and historical interest.

This publication is made possible through the Marilyn Schneider Memorial Fund. Marilyn, one of the Foundation's first docents, gave unstintingly of her time and energy until her death in 1974. This, then, is a monument to her.

INTRODUCTION

You'll like Graceland. If you're interested in art and architecture, if you're a Chicago history buff, if you like stories about famous people, or if you're only looking for a little peace and quiet in the busy city, you'll like Graceland.

It has statues by famed sculptors Lorado Taft and Daniel Chester French. It has mausoleums designed by renowned architects. The masterpiece is the tomb that Louis Sullivan designed for Carrie Eliza Getty. This Chicago landmark has been described as the beginning of modern architecture in America.

The men who built Chicago — literally built it — lie here: Louis Sullivan himself, his fellow architects Daniel Burnham and John Root and a modern-day colleague, Ludwig Mies van der Rohe.

Buried here are many of early Chicago's most prominent citizens, people whose names still echo in the city: Marshall Field, Potter Palmer, George Pullman, Cyrus McCormick, Philip Armour. These and so many more whose names will be familiar to you rest in this quiet green place. The tale of how they rose from young pioneers to wealthy civic leaders is the story of Chicago itself, the city that began as a cluster of structures in the mud of the river bank and became the booming center of the nation's industry, transportation and trade.

History of Graceland

Graceland Cemetery was established in 1860 and received a perpetual charter from the State of Illinois in 1861. Its southern boundary (now Irving Park Road) was two miles outside city limits. The western boundary (now Clark Street) was Green Bay Road, an old Indian trail and, once upon a time, the shore of Lake Michigan. The land along this natural ridge is high ground and therefore appropriate for a burial place.

Thomas Bryan bought the land and founded Graceland. He was a Harvard-trained lawyer from Virginia who had established a successful practice in the city. He also built Bryan Hall, where meetings and entertainments were held, established a Soldiers Home and served as a director of the Columbian Exposition, the World's Fair of 1893. In fact, he was involved in the campaign to have Chicago chosen as the Fair site.

1

Bryan acted as president of the cemetery company. A board of managers consisted of several prominent Chicagoans. Among them was real-estate entrepreneur William Ogden, the city's first mayor. Most of the other well-to-do Chicagoans bought spacious plots and became members of the cemetery company.

In the beginning, Graceland covered 80 acres. Its state charter gave the company the right to acquire up to 500 additional acres. By the late 1860s, the cemetery had bought 200 acres in the surrounding area, which it planned to incorporate as burial ground. However, residents of the area, the town of Lake View, protested. They passed amendments to their town charter forbidding Graceland to use for cemeterial purposes any grounds not already enclosed within the cemetery walls. Graceland, in turn, protested that the town could not supersede the cemetery's state charter.

What threatened to become a court case was settled by compromise. Graceland gave up its unoccupied lands and expansion plans for some land adjacent to its eastern boundary and at its northwest corner. This filled out the cemetery to its roughly rectangular area of 119 acres.

An early design for Graceland had been the work of landscape architect H. W. S. Cleveland. In the 1870s, in accordance with that plan, the paths as well as the plots were sodded to produce a uniform surface. The practice of marking off plot boundaries with low fences or with coping (stone curbing) was no longer allowed.

After the additional land became part of the cemetery, park designer and landscape architect Ossian Simonds was asked to create a lasting plan for Graceland. His innovative design relied on the use of native plants to create a naturalistic landscape.

Simonds had been consulting landscape designer for Lincoln Park and was a founder and partner of the architectural firm of Holabird, Simonds & Roche. He withdrew from the firm in 1883 to begin his lifelong association with Graceland.

Holabird & Roche designed all the buildings for the cemetery: the crematorium, the chapel (the original portion), the waiting room and office and the entrance (the present gates are not the original ones). The buildings are low and nestled into the contours of the landscape, in keeping with Graceland's park-like design.

Victorian Cemetery

The concept of making a cemetery like a park goes back to Queen Victoria's England. The Victorians developed this kind of cemetery in reaction to horrible burial conditions.

In the early 1800s, more and more people were leaving the English countryside to find work in the cities. The cities became vastly overcrowded. Poverty, disease and early death were common. The poor were buried in cheap coffins that often fell apart before they were put into the ground. In the public graveyards, more than a dozen coffins might be placed in a grave, one on top of the other with no earth in between.

In the churchyard cemeteries, conditions were no better. Shortly after burial, corpses would be disinterred and burned to make room for new burials. Graves often lay open, plundered by robbers. Because of such sights, not to mention the smell of decaying matter, burial grounds were thoroughly unpleasant places.

The Victorians turned their energies to changing all that, and the result was the spacious, park-like cemetery — a lovely, green area which could provide a resting place for the living as well as the dead.

Conditions in Chicago

In the 1850s in rapidly-growing Chicago, cemetery conditions may not have been desperate, but new burial grounds were needed. The city's lakefront public cemetery was becoming dangerously overcrowded. Epidemics of water-borne diseases such as typhoid and cholera were claiming increasing numbers of victims. The city drew its water supply from the lake, but slaughterhouses and distilleries dumped their refuse into the river . . . which emptied into the lake.

In 1858, a petition signed by City Cemetery neighbors and the championing of their cause by Dr. John Rauch focused attention on the unhealthy conditions.

Dr. Rauch spoke before civic groups, urging that the graves in the overcrowded cemetery be moved and the area turned into a park.

In 1864, the Chicago City Council set aside the land as Lake Park (later renamed Lincoln Park in honor of the assassinated President) and decreed that the graves be moved to private cemeteries, such as Graceland.

1. ELI WILLIAMS   1799-1881

The starting point of our walk is the grave of one of the early settlers of Chicago. Eli Williams came here from Connecticut in the early 1830s when the population was about 200. He ran a store, made money in the booming real estate market, built a hotel, took an active part in civic affairs and died a wealthy man. He's representative of the enterprising, adventurous pioneers who came here from the East or the South to make their fortunes when they and Chicago were young.

Williams' first wife, who died in Connecticut, is buried on one side of him. His second wife lies on the other. Also buried here is his son, Hobart, who left an estate of $5 million when he died in 1921.

On the north side of the plot you'll find the small markers for two daughters who died in infancy. The infant-mortality rate was very high. This fact probably was an important impetus in the cemetery reform movement in the 1800s. Victorian mothers, whose children often died young, wanted to be sure that their little ones would lie undisturbed.

The vine-covered statue of a woman holding a cross is a good example of Victorian cemetery memorials. Along with their movement to reform cemeteries, the Victorians placed a great emphasis on the ceremonies surrounding death. Lavish funerals became the rule, and sentimental figures such as this one were often part of the extravagant memorials erected over the graves.

2. DEXTER GRAVES   1789-1844

The bronze figure — often called the *Statue of Death* — was entitled *Eternal Silence* by its creator, sculptor Lorado Taft, whose monumental *Fountain of Time* still stands at the west end of the University of Chicago Midway. At the base of the statue are Taft's signature and the year of completion, 1909.

Eternal Silence marks the burial plot of the Graves family. Dexter Graves, a hotel owner in early Chicago, was, like Eli Williams, among the first settlers in the area. According to the inscription on the back of the polished black granite slab, Graves "brought the first colony to Chicago, consisting of 13 families, arriving here July 15, 1831, from Ashtabula, Ohio, on the schooner *Telegraph.*"

The hooded figure is as grim and forbidding a picture of death as one would wish to see. We'll compare it later with another attitude toward death, the one expressed by Daniel Chester French in his monument for Marshall Field.

Just south of *Eternal Silence* is the Jenney plot. Engineer-architect William Le Baron Jenney invented the skyscraper. In the Home Insurance Building, which he built in 1884, Jenney pioneered the use of the skeleton frame and forever changed the course of architecture. The 10-story Home Insurance Building, the world's first skyscraper, stood at the northeast corner of LaSalle and Adams until it was demolished in 1931.

Jenney died in 1907 during a visit to California. His body was cremated and his ashes returned to Chicago to be sprinkled near his wife's grave in the family plot here at Graceland.

3. JOHN KINZIE   1763-1828

Here are the very beginnings of Chicago history. The words on the stone are somewhat faded, for this limestone marker has withstood a century and a half of Chicago weather. The modern headstone in front of it bears a clearer inscription. It records the name, date of birth and date of death of trader John Kinzie, the first permanent white settler of Chicago. Kinzie was born before the Revolutionary War. His slab headstone and footstone date back further than any of the other grave markers here.

A native of Quebec, Kinzie came to the area in 1804. He and his family settled across the Chicago River from the newly-built Fort Dearborn in the homestead that Jean Baptiste Du Sable had built (about where the Equitable Building is now).

Indian trader Du Sable, a black man from the West Indies, was Chicago's first permanent settler. He had arrived around 1779 and over the years built up quite a substantial establishment on the river, including house, dairy, smokehouse, stables and barn. He sold the place in 1800 and moved to Peoria.

Kinzie and his family remained until 1812. After war was declared against the British in that year, the occupants of Fort Dearborn and the

surrounding area were ordered to evacuate. As they did so, they were massacred by the Indians. The Kinzies, however, escaped to Michigan. Although the Indians burned the fort, they spared the Kinzie home. The area was largely deserted until 1816 when the fort was rebuilt and the Kinzie family returned.

When Kinzie died in 1828, he was buried in the Fort Dearborn cemetery. Later, he was moved to the city burial grounds on the north side and then, as the expanding city once more established a new burial ground, to the lakefront cemetery. When Lincoln Park was developed there, he was moved again, this time to the Kinzie plot here in Graceland.

Our next stop is the grave of boxer Robert Fitzsimmons, but before we get there, we'll pass Mausoleum Row.

The word *mausoleum* derives from the name of King Mausolus, ancient ruler of a country in southwestern Asia Minor (present-day Turkey). When Mausolus died, around 350 B.C., his widow built him a splendid tomb at Halicarnassus. It was the first mausoleum and, in fact, one of the seven wonders of the ancient world.

Today, any large and imposing tomb to hold coffins or funeral urns is a mausoleum. You can see from the ones along the road on your right that they may vary as to material (granite, limestone) and style (Egyptian, Greek, Roman, etc.).

Tombs, just like any other structure, often followed whatever style happened to be in fashion. Of course, the choice also depended upon the client's wealth and good taste. The people buried here generally seem to have had a fair amount of both.

Take a minute to look inside and around these mausoleums. Some have beautiful stained glass windows.

Just before you get to the Espert tomb, turn right and walk across the grass to find Fitzsimmons' headstone.

4. ROBERT FITZSIMMONS   1862-1917

Boxing champion Fitzsimmons, an Englishman who grew up in New Zealand, had the distinction of winning titles in three divisions. In 1891, he won the middleweight title. On St. Patrick's Day in 1897, he became the heavyweight champion by knocking out Irishman James J. Corbett. Fitzsimmons, who weighed only about 160 pounds, floored Corbett with his famous solar plexus punch. In 1903, he won the light-heavyweight title.

The original Fitzsimmons headstone was replaced by a red granite one in 1973. An article about the boxer in the *Chicago Daily News* had prompted a reader to call the newspaper's attention to the fact that Fitzsimmons' name was misspelled on his headstone (the middle *s* was missing). The newspaper contacted the Veteran Boxers Association of Illinois, and this organization of old-time boxers and boxing fans arranged for the new stone. The photographs on the original stone were carefully transferred. The red granite is quite appropriate: one of the redheaded Fitzsimmons' nicknames was "Ruby Robert."

5. JACK JOHNSON   1878-1946

On Christmas Day in 1908, Johnson knocked out Tommy Burns in a prizefight in Australia and became the first black boxer to win the world heavyweight championship. He lost the title in 1915 to Jess Willard in a 26-round fight in Cuba. Johnson said later that he threw the fight to get back into the good graces of those who hated him. Hated him because he dared to marry a white woman. Whites had searched everywhere for someone — "the great white hope" — to beat him.

Johnson died after an auto accident near Raleigh, N.C., in 1946. He lies in the family plot he purchased in 1912 for the burial of his wife, Etta. A large stone bears the name "Johnson." In front of it, to one side, is a small headstone with the inscription, "Etta, beloved wife of Jack A. Johnson, 1881-1912." Johnson is buried next to Etta, but his grave is unmarked.

In 1969, the cast of *The Great White Hope* came to Graceland in chartered buses, brought flowers and listened to a eulogy by the actor who was portraying the fighter. The group had also planned to put a headstone on Johnson's grave, but the family objected, calling the whole thing a callous public relations stunt.

6. VICTOR LAWSON 1850-1925

Lorado Taft sculpted this larger-than-life *Crusader* in 1931 for the grave of newspaper publisher Victor Fremont Lawson. Lawson's *Chicago Daily News* was a paper that took pride in its political independence and its factual reporting. It was the first paper west of New York to sell for only a penny. Its Chicago competitors cost three or five cents.

Melville Stone established the *Chicago Daily News* in 1875, publishing his first issue on Dec. 23. He rented quarters in the office of *The Scandinavian,* a newspaper that Lawson's father had helped found. After six months, Stone's two partners sold out and Lawson, 22, bought their interest. Stone continued as editor while Lawson handled the business matters. In 1888, Lawson bought out Stone and remained sole owner and publisher until his death in 1925.

Lawson pioneered in sending reporters to distant parts of the world for news. He established a chain of correspondents that became the Daily News Foreign Service.

His paper established the Fresh Air Fund, which maintained a sanitarium at Lincoln Park for sick underprivileged children. He contributed generously — and usually anonymously — to the YMCA and a number of charitable causes. Indeed, Lawson's name cannot be found here either. His grave is unmarked, except for that splendid crusading knight.

The Kroeschells' rough-edged marker, across the road from Lawson's grave, looks as if part of it might have been torn away by some inexplicable force. No, it started out this way. This kind of monument symbolizes that a life has been broken, torn asunder by death.

Near the Kroeschell plot is the Hutchinson monument decorated with a bronze bas-relief, *A Man of Sorrows.* Charles Hutchinson was a banker and the first president of the Art Institute. The panel is signed in the lower right corner by its sculptor, A. Faggi. The work, with its Christ figure, is similar to the Stations of the Cross that Faggi did for the church of St. Thomas the Apostle on the city's south side.

ABOVE ALL THINGS TRUTH
BEARETH AWAY THE VICTORY

7. JOHN ROOT 1850-91

Southerner John Wellborn Root came to Chicago in 1871 with a degree in civil engineering and a year's experience in a New York architectural firm. He became a draftsman in a firm here, made friends with co-worker Daniel Burnham, and the two started their own firm in 1873. Root did the design work and Burnham, an excellent organizer, handled the business end. There wasn't much of it in the first lean years, but Burnham & Root eventually emerged as one of the finest firms in the city. Unfortunately, many of their buildings are gone, but two that do remain — the charming Rookery on LaSalle Street and the unadorned Monadnock at Dearborn and Jackson — exemplify their best work.

In the 16-story Monadnock, Burnham and Root pushed the old technology as far as it could go. It was the tallest building that could be built with load-bearing walls, walls that carried the weight of the structure. The walls had to be six feet at the base to be strong enough to support the building.

The logical alternative was the skeleton frame, introduced by William Le Baron Jenney in 1884 in the Home Insurance Building. With a steel skeleton frame to support a building, the wall could become a mere curtain. It was left to the talents of Holabird, Roche, Burnham, Root and Louis Sullivan to experiment with the new technology and develop an exterior style to go with it, a style that would express the building's function.

These men were in the forefront of what came to be called the Chicago School of Architecture. It was not a school in the literal sense, of course. It was a group of architects who, instead of adhering to tradition and looking to the past for architectural models, used a new technology — iron and steel, a skeleton frame, fireproofing, the elevator — to create a new kind of building, the skyscraper.

John Root was an important part of the Chicago School, but his role ended abruptly. He died of pneumonia at the age of 41, just as he and Burnham were beginning to get involved in planning for the Columbian Exposition of 1893.

Root had spent his career breaking away from architectural tradition, but his Graceland monument is wholly traditional. Members of his firm

14

designed a Celtic cross because he had admired those he had seen in English cemeteries. Charles Atwood chose as a model the crosses left by the Druids, and Jules Wegman did the design work. Although Celtic crosses were usually carved in sandstone, this one was done in a more durable red Scottish granite so it could better withstand Chicago's climate. A panel on the face of the cross contains one of Root's drawings, the entrance to the Phoenix Building (demolished in 1959).

8. PETER SCHOENHOFEN 1827-93

This pyramid was built for a wealthy brewer. Peter Schoenhofen, born in Prussia, emigrated when he was 24. He and a partner established a brewery in Chicago in 1860. When his partner withdrew seven years later, Schoenhofen continued the business as the Schoenhofen Brewing Company. At the time, the German population of the city was increasing rapidly and a number of breweries were being established. Schoenhofen's prospered and by the 1880s was one of the largest. The brewery was on the northwest corner of 18th and Canalport. A building designed for the company in 1902 by architect Richard Schmidt still occupies that site.

The sphinx and angel guarding the entrance of Schoenhofen's pyramid are a rather unlikely pair. The angel, a Christian symbol and a typical figure on Victorian monuments, seems out of place on this imitation of an ancient Egyptian pyramid. The Egyptians were worshippers of the sun. For them, the pyramid represented the setting sun and the coming of darkness and death. It served as a tomb for royalty.

As you walk through Graceland, you'll see a number of obelisks, another monument that goes back to ancient Egypt. The obelisk represented a ray of light, a sunbeam. It symbolized the sun at its zenith and marked the grave of a king.

9. GEORGE PULLMAN   1831-97

The monument for the inventor of the Pullman sleeping car is a good place to rest. It's an exedra, which means it has seats. In ancient Greece, an exedra was an outdoor bench where scholars might gather.

Solon Beman designed this monument with its stately Corinthian column. But what's underneath the monument is much more unusual. Pullman's coffin, covered in tar paper and asphalt, is sunk in a concrete block the size of a room. The top of the block is overlaid with railroad ties and more concrete. George Pullman is down there to stay.

Why this remarkably thorough method of burial? The family thought it necessary to protect Pullman's body from angry workers.

A brief but bitter strike against Pullman had occurred in 1894. The 1893 economic depression had caused Pullman to cut wages at his Pullman Palace Car Company. However, he did not cut rents for his workers, who lived in the company town that he had hired Solon Beman to build. Since Pullman deducted the rents from employees' salaries, most of them ended up with little pay or none at all.

When Pullman refused to negotiate about their complaints, his workers went out on strike. They gained the support across the nation of the young American Railway Union, led by Eugene Debs. The strikers refused to allow Pullman cars to be included in the trains, and the railroads refused to run without them.

The railroad managers went to U.S. Attorney General Richard Olney, a former lawyer for the railroads, for help in quelling the strike and defeating the fledgling union. They argued that the strikers were interfering with the transport of the U.S. mail. Olney persuaded President Grover Cleveland to send in federal troops. When Cleveland did, the strike ended quickly, but the bitterness and anger remained. Most Pullman workers lost their jobs; all new employees were required to pledge that they would not join a union.

In the plot next to Pullman's are his daughter Florence and her husband, Frank Lowden, who was governor of Illinois from 1917-21.

18

10. MARTIN RYERSON   1818-87

Ryerson was a teenager when he left his New Jersey home to go west. He got as far as Michigan, where he became an Indian fur trader, then a general store clerk and, finally, a sawmill owner. About 1850, he opened an office in Chicago for his growing lumber business and established his home here. Within the next twenty years, Chicago became the distribution center for the nation's lumber trade.

After making a fortune in lumber, Ryerson made another in real estate. During the 1880s, Adler & Sullivan built four office buildings for Ryerson. When he died in 1887, his son, Martin A. Ryerson, commissioned Louis Sullivan to design the tomb.

For one of the office buildings, the young Sullivan had designed ornament somewhat Egyptian in style. For the tomb, Sullivan turned for inspiration to Egyptian burial monuments — the pyramid and its forerunner, the mastaba, a block-like structure with a flat top and slanted sides.

Sullivan combined the two forms into the massive solidity of the Ryerson monument. The tomb, made of polished black granite, appears as timeless and immutable as its models. You might want to look more closely at a few details that offer a nice contrast to all the strong, straight lines — the pattern of leaves on the lock of the bronze gate and the flower-like design of the grating over the back window.

Sullivan designed three tombs in his career, and two of them are in Graceland. The Ryerson was the first. The Getty tomb, done a year later, is not far from here. The Wainwright tomb, finished in 1892, is in St. Louis' Bellefontaine Cemetery.

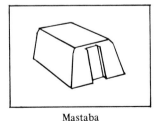

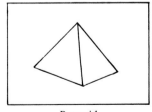

Mastaba   Pyramid

20

11. LOUIS SULLIVAN   1856-1924

Louis Sullivan, buried here with his parents, is commonly ranked as one of the best architects this country ever produced. Through his theories, expressed in his buildings and his writings, he helped to create modern architecture. But in the last five years of his life, he received only one commission. When he died, he was poor, ill, alone and all but forgotten − except by one man who had been an apprentice in Sullivan's firm, Frank Lloyd Wright.

The beginning had been quite different. Sullivan, the boy wonder, became a full partner with Dankmar Adler at the age of 24. One of their most important commissions was the Auditorium, which still stands as a tribute to Adler's engineering genius and Sullivan's gift for creating exquisite ornament.

Sullivan's Auditorium design was influenced by a recently finished Henry Hobson Richardson building, a wholesale store for Marshall Field. That building no longer exists; it long since had to make way for a parking lot. But it was an example of Richardson's individualism, his ability to take what he wanted from architecture of the past and turn it to suit his own style. Through its influence on Sullivan and his contemporaries, it helped start an architectural revolution.

Sullivan became the leader of the Chicago School, forging the way in developing a new architecture, one that did not rely upon the precedents of the past but responded to the technology and human needs of the day.

Among Sullivan's finest designs is the Carson Pirie Scott store, one of the few Sullivan buildings left in the Loop. The facade with its large rectangles of windows gives clear indication of the steel skeleton underneath, and the lovely ornament framing the display windows and the rounded corner entrance is unequaled.

But suddenly Sullivan was no longer in demand. The planners of the 1893 World's Fair rejected the innovations of the Chicago School for the more respectable models of the past. Their bow to classicism set an example that was followed for many years.

About five years after his death, some recognition came to Louis Sullivan in the form of this headstone. A committee headed by architect Thomas Tallmadge planned the memorial and financed it with private contributions. An architectural historian as well as an architect, Tallmadge coined the term *Chicago School* to identify the work of Sullivan and his colleagues. He wrote the tribute engraved on the back of the stone. The sculptured sides of the rough granite symbolize the development of the skyscraper. On the front, Sullivan's profile is set against one of his own designs.

12. WILLIAM KIMBALL   1828-1904

A native of Maine, Kimball visited Chicago in 1857 as a traveling salesman. Impressed with the city's vitality, he entered into business here as a wholesale dealer in pianos and organs. Kimball was confident that, as the area became more settled, interest in music and the arts would grow. By 1881, he was successful enough to open an organ factory. Six years later, his company began making pianos, too.

Kimball's classical monument was designed by McKim, Mead & White, an East Coast firm that had participated in creating the impressive classical buildings for the 1893 Fair.

The weatherworn limestone memorial is across the road from George Pullman's monument. Kimball and Pullman are neighbors here, just as they were on Prairie Avenue. Near them in this fashionable lakeside area of Graceland lie others who once lived in Prairie Avenue mansions: Peter Schoenhofen, Philip Armour, John Glessner and Marshall Field. After the Chicago Fire of 1871, Prairie Avenue became the fashionable place to live, the Gold Coast of its day.

The Kimballs' mansion still occupies the southeast corner of 18th and Prairie. Designed for them by Solon Beman and built in 1892, it cost $1 million. It stands across the street from the home that Henry Richardson designed for John Glessner in 1885.

These two houses and others on the street are to be preserved, thanks to the creation of the Prairie Avenue Historical District. The purpose of the district is to preserve not only architecture but historical, cultural, and social elements as well. The streetscape, for example, has been restored to its 1890s appearance, right down to the sidewalks, curbs, hitching posts, trees and gas lights. The district also encompasses the site of the Fort Dearborn massacre and is home to the Widow Clarke House, which was built in the 1830s and is the oldest Chicago residence still standing.

24

13. WILLIAM GOODMAN   1848-1936

Goodman, like Martin Ryerson, was a lumber magnate. He had this mausoleum built for his playwright son, Kenneth Sawyer Goodman, who died at the age of 35. Kenneth was a naval lieutenant in training at Great Lakes Naval Training Station when, in 1918, he became a victim of the influenza epidemic.

William Goodman's close friend, architect Howard Van Doren Shaw, designed the tomb. A fittingly dramatic resting place it is, rising out of the sheltering hillside, with an entrance directly on the water and a roof balcony overlooking the lake. There's a good view of its neoclassical facade from across the lake at the grave of Ludwig Mies van der Rohe.

Shaw used the same architectural style in 1925 when he designed the Goodman Theatre, which the William Goodmans founded as a memorial to their dramatist son.

14. POTTER PALMER   1826-1902

A lovely surprise awaits you as you leave the Goodman tomb and walk past the row of bushes. At the top of a rise, overlooking the lake, sits a Greek temple. Potter and Bertha Palmer lie at rest here in the same grand style and sumptuous splendor in which they lived . . . proving, perhaps, that you really can take it with you after all.

Young Potter Palmer had operated a dry-goods store in his native New York before coming to Chicago to make his fortune. He opened a store on Lake Street, then the center of Chicago's commercial activity, and made it a success with his unusual methods. He gave customers their money back if they weren't satisfied with a purchase, he allowed people to take merchandise home on approval, he advertised widely and he insisted on attractive store displays.

Having made a fortune, he sold his store to Marshall Field and Levi Leiter and turned to real estate. He bought State Street, widened it,

constructed new buildings all along it and transformed it into the new commercial center of the city. And on it, he built a luxurious hotel, the Palmer House. In the year he was married, he gave the hotel to his young bride, Kentucky-bred Bertha Honoré, as a wedding present. But the year was 1871. In October, the Palmer House as well as much else in the city was destroyed by the Great Fire. Undaunted, Palmer borrowed money and rebuilt the street, complete with another, even more impressive Palmer House.

Then he proceeded to make the city's near north side the successor to the south side's Prairie Avenue as the enclave of the wealthy. He had the marshy land filled in and built a splendid castle on Lake Shore Drive. From here, his wife ruled as queen of Chicago society. This was the setting for Bertha Palmer's lavish entertainments and for her unrivaled collection of French Impressionist paintings, which she later donated to the Art Institute.

McKim, Mead & White designed the Palmers' temple with its twin sarcophagi, or stone coffins. (The word *sarcophagus* comes from the Greek, *to eat flesh*. It was thus applied because the material used by the Greeks for a sarcophagus — limestone — caused a rapid disintegration of its contents.)

Across the road are real-estate tycoon Henry Hamilton Honoré and his wife, Bertha Palmer's parents. McKim, Mead & White also designed their charming Gothic tomb — French Gothic, in keeping with the ancestry of the Honorés.

15. CHARLES WACKER   1856-1929

This is the man for whom Wacker Drive is named. He was thus honored because of his work as chairman of the Chicago Plan Commission. The commission was formed by civic leaders to win public acceptance for Daniel Burnham's Chicago Plan of 1909.

Burnham's plan was a blueprint for the orderly growth and development of the city. Burnham outlined, for example, plans for the

30

arrangement of streets and highways, the construction of railway terminals and the establishment of a ring of parks connected by broad boulevards. Another of his proposals called for a double-decked road around the Loop to relieve traffic congestion.

As commission chairman, Wacker worked hard to educate people about the plan and to win public support — and tax money — for it. When part of the plan — a double-decked road on the south bank of the river — was completed, it was given Wacker's name in recognition of his efforts.

Turn right at Wacker's tomb and go east across the grass, almost to the road on the other side. You'll find John Altgeld's marker next to a white birch tree.

16. JOHN ALTGELD   1847-1902

John Peter Altgeld — lawyer, judge and author of a book on prison reform — served as governor of Illinois from 1893-97. The bronze plaques on the stout shaft which marks his grave contain excerpts from his public statements. The two most notable quotations are his pardon of the Haymarket anarchists in 1893 and his protest to President Cleveland against sending federal troops to Illinois during the Pullman strike of 1894. These statements made Altgeld the object of abuse and scorn across the country and ended his political career.

The Haymarket Riot had occurred in strike-ridden Chicago on May 4, 1886. Anarchists called a mass meeting to protest police brutality. On the previous day at the McCormick plant, several people had been killed when police intervened in a fight between strikers and the strikebreakers who were operating the plant under police guard.

The gathering at Haymarket Square was tame enough until the police ordered the crowd to disperse. A bomb was thrown and shooting began. Seven policemen were killed and more than 60 wounded.

Eight known anarchists were brought to trial. The identity of the bomb-thrower was never established, but the eight were found guilty because they had made speeches advocating violence. Four of the men were hanged, and one committed suicide in his cell. The other three were imprisoned.

In 1893, lawyer Clarence Darrow and others approached Altgeld about a pardon for the three. After reviewing the case, Altgeld became convinced the trial had been unfair and he granted the pardons. Then the storm broke. Across the country, Altgeld was burned in effigy and vilified in the press, particularly Joseph Medill's *Chicago Tribune.*

In 1894, during the Pullman strike, Altgeld again took a principled stand that made him many enemies. The state militia was maintaining order during the strike, but President Cleveland was persuaded by the railroad managers to send in federal troops. Altgeld protested that the act was an unwarranted usurpation of power by the President. For this stand, as in the case of the Haymarket pardons, he was labeled an anarchist and a radical and was never again elected to public office.

Return to the Wacker monument and then follow the curve of the road to Edith McCormick's grave. On the way, notice the Holmes mausoleum. With its strong vertical lines and geometric patterns, it's a good example of the Art Deco style. Art Deco took its name from the 1925 *Exposition International des Arts Decoratifs et Industriels Modernes* in Paris, where it was first exhibited.

The style is based on geometric forms. The goal of those who developed it was to adapt design to the machine age, to the conditions of mass production. Art Deco permeated every area of life in the '20s and '30s, and it enjoyed a revival in the late '60s and early '70s. The style was used in designing glassware, jewelry, posters, furniture and textiles as well as buildings. (A lovely Art Deco example in the Loop is the lobby of the Board of Trade at the foot of LaSalle Street.)

17. EDITH ROCKEFELLER McCORMICK   1872-1932

Edith was the daughter of John D. Rockefeller and the daughter-in-law of Cyrus McCormick. One would not know from this modest grave that her wealth had once been estimated at between $50 million and $100 million. However, when she died in 1932, the undertaker had to present a claim to collect his money for the expensive casket. Edith had owned a million dollars' worth of jewels, had supported the opera generously and had been the successor to Bertha Palmer as the queen of Chicago society. She died virtually penniless as a result of the Depression, lavish spending and heavy investments in unsound real estate projects.

Her funeral services were held in her mansion on Lake Shore Drive while thousands jammed the streets outside to see the funeral procession. Her casket was placed in an underground vault at Graceland alongside the coffins of two of her children.

Edith and her husband, Harold, were divorced in 1921. Harold married twice more, died in 1941 and was buried in Los Angeles. In June, 1953, his casket was unearthed, flown to Chicago and buried here in Graceland — on the other side of the lake, next to his father, Cyrus. At the same time, the caskets of Edith and the children were taken from the vault and buried here on this side of the lake. Besides the workmen, the only person present for the burials was Edith and Harold's son, Fowler, who had very quietly arranged it all. Now Fowler, too, is dead and buried with his father and grandfather.

18. DANIEL BURNHAM   1846-1912

Daniel Burnham was partners with architect John Root, whose grave we saw earlier. Root's untimely death occurred as planning was getting under way for the 1893 Columbian Exposition. Deeply saddened by the loss of his friend, Burnham threw himself into the Fair preparations. As chief of construction for the event, he ably coordinated the work of creating the awesome White City on Chicago's south side. A remnant of its splendor still exists there; the building housing the Museum of Science and Industry was originally built by Burnham's firm for the Fair.

After the Fair, D. H. Burnham & Company was increasingly busy. The Reliance Building, the Fisher Building, the Railway Exchange Building and the Marshall Field store are some of that period's commissions still standing in the Loop. But Burnham soon began turning his energies to city planning. In his famed Chicago Plan of 1909, he created one of the most comprehensive guides to city development. "Make no little plans," was his dictum. "They have no magic to stir men's blood . . . ."

As part of his plan, Burnham proposed that the city's lakefront be preserved for the enjoyment and recreational use of its citizens. The park system that lines the lake today is a result of his vision. Thus, it seems particularly fitting that his final resting place be on this pleasant, wooded isle in the lake at Graceland.

19. LUDWIG WOLFF   1836-1911

This bunker of a tomb, three-quarters below ground, belongs to a man who manufactured all kinds of copper and brass work, including plumbing supplies and equipment for brewers, distillers and candy-makers.

Wolff was a coppersmith's apprentice in his native Germany. He and his family came to this country in 1854. Cholera broke out on the boat during their voyage over and killed hundreds of passengers. Shortly after arriving, Wolff's parents and three of his brothers also died. He was left with the care of four younger children.

He worked as a coppersmith until 1856, when he started a company in partnership with a plumber, Terence McGuire. He bought his partner's interest ten years later and became sole proprietor.

20. GETTY TOMB   1890

In this place of beautiful and striking monuments, here stands the finest
of them all — the Getty tomb. Lumber merchant Henry Harrison Getty
commissioned Sullivan to design this tomb when Getty's wife, Carrie
Eliza, died. Getty, a partner of Martin Ryerson, knew the work Sullivan
had done for Ryerson — the Loop office buildings as well as the
pyramid mausoleum. Getty himself died in 1919 and is buried here, as
is the couple's only child, Alice, who died in 1946.

The tomb stands apart on its own little triangle of land, just as it stands
apart from the other monuments in the cemetery in its historic and
architectural significance. In recognition of that significance, it was
formally designated a city landmark in 1971. The plaque in front of it
bears the following inscription from the Commission on Chicago
Historical and Architectural Landmarks:

> The Getty Tomb marks the maturity of Sullivan's
> architectural style and the beginning of modern
> architecture in America. Here the architect departed
> from historic precedent to create a building of strong
> geometric massing, detailed with original ornament.

Such a heavy responsibility for this tomb to bear: "the beginning of
modern architecture in America." But the citation justly acknowledges
Sullivan's originality. The Ryerson tomb was his variation on an
Egyptian burial monument. To create the graceful Getty tomb, Sullivan
looked not to architectural models of the past, not to precedents, but
into his own imagination.

The result — a delicately ornamented cube uniquely suited to its
purpose as a woman's last resting place. It deserves close examination.

The bottom half of each wall is smooth, the top half decorated with
octagons containing eight-pointed, star-like designs. In the arches over
the door and two side windows, bands of smooth stone alternate with
ornamented bands. In front and at the back of the tomb, the top edge
of the cornice is straight; on the two sides, it's scalloped. The bottom
edge of the cornice is banded with ornament. Perhaps, in the worn
limestone, the rich ornament is not etched as sharply as it once was —
this tomb has been standing here since before the turn of the century,

38

remember — but it's still possible to trace the intricacy of the flower-leaf patterns.

The bronze gate and the door behind it, gone green with time, are masterpieces. The star-like design of the walls is here lavishly interlaced with geometric and floral forms. A full-size plaster cast of the doorway was exhibited in the Paris Exposition of 1900 and earned Sullivan an award. Take a look at one more detail. Notice how Sullivan worked Getty's initials into a medallion in the windows.

21. JOSEPH MEDILL   1823-99

The first in this row of solid conventional tombstones belongs to the Medill family.

Joseph Medill was first a lawyer and then a newspaper publisher in Ohio before he came to Chicago. He became part owner and editor of the *Chicago Tribune* in 1855.

Medill — as well as his newspaper — was staunchly conservative, Republican, anti-slavery and anti-labor-union. He had been a founder of the Republican party and an early supporter of Abraham Lincoln. It was largely through Medill's wheeling and dealing at the 1860 Republican convention in Chicago that Lincoln won the nomination for President.

Medill eventually went into politics himself. After the Chicago Fire, he was elected mayor on the "fireproof" ticket. He enforced stringent fire regulations during the rebuilding of the city, and he helped to establish the Chicago Public Library. He also made the vastly unpopular move of closing the saloons on Sunday. In the great swell of protest that followed, the law was repealed. Mayor Medill resigned before his term was up and went off to Europe to rest.

When Medill returned in 1874, he assumed full control of the *Tribune*. Upon his death, more than two decades later, it passed to his heirs — the Pattersons and the McCormicks. One of Medill's daughters had married a Patterson; another, a nephew of Cyrus McCormick.

22. LAMBERT TREE   1832-1910

Tree was a lawyer, judge and diplomat. When he became a circuit court judge in 1870, he initiated a grand-jury investigation of corruption in the Chicago City Council, leading to the trial and conviction of many council members. In 1885, President Cleveland appointed Tree U.S. minister to Belgium. In 1888, he was named minister to Russia.

23. PHILIP ARMOUR   1832-1901

Is there anyone who doesn't recognize the name on this tombstone? It's a name commonly seen on cans and packages of meat products all over the world.

Philip Armour didn't settle in Chicago until 1875, when he came here to take over a grain business and a meat-packing company from an ailing brother. Before that, he was a partner with John Plankinton in a Milwaukee pork-packing plant.

Armour and Plankinton made a name for themselves — and a fortune of $1.5 million — when they sold short in the last months of the Civil War. Gambling that the war would end soon and pork prices would fall, Armour went to New York and contracted to sell pork for future delivery at $40 a barrel. When, indeed, prices did drop, Armour was able to buy for only $18 a barrel all the pork needed to meet the firm's commitments.

In Chicago, Armour and such competitors as Swift and Libby became the barons of the meat-packing industry, centered in the Union Stock Yards on the south side. Railroad lines brought the livestock directly into the yards and then took the dressed meat out in refrigerated cars. Not only the meat, but innumerable by-products, such as soap, gelatin and jewelry. The Chicago packers used all the pig but the squeal, it was said. And the city became the meat-packing center of the country, "hog-butcher of the world," as Carl Sandburg later described it.

In the 1950s that was no longer true and the meat-packing companies were moving elsewhere. The Armour plant here closed in 1959. But an Armour legacy remains in the city. Philip Armour once gave $1 million to a young minister after he heard the man preach a sermon entitled, "What I Would Do with a Million Dollars." What he did do, with Armour's help, was build a technical school for young men, the Armour Institute. Founded in 1893, it later merged with Lewis Institute to form the Illinois Institute of Technology.

24. LUCIUS FISHER   1843-1916

Fisher was born in Beloit, Wis. (His father was a founder of Beloit College.) He fought for the Union during the Civil War and settled in Chicago when it was over. He became involved in a number of businesses, including the Union Bag & Paper Company, of which he was president, and the Exhaust Ventilator Company, which he founded. His extensive real estate interests included the Fisher Building, at Van Buren and Dearborn, built for him by D. H. Burnham & Company.

The man who designed a north addition to that building, Peter J. Weber, also designed the Fisher columbarium here in Graceland. A columbarium is a vault to hold urns containing the ashes of cremated bodies; the word comes from the Latin word for dovecote.

The bronze hooded angel holding an urn was sculpted by Richard Bock. His name is at the bottom right. Bock specialized in architectural decoration and military memorials.

25. JOHN GLESSNER   1843-1936

Vice president of a harvesting machine company in Springfield, Ohio, Glessner moved here in 1870 to establish a Chicago office for the firm. He later became a vice president of the International Harvester Company.

The grave markers for Glessner, his wife and one of their children, who died in infancy, are less imposing than many others here. What is special about the Glessners is not the place where they lie buried, but the place where they lived.

Their remarkable house still stands on the corner of Prairie Avenue and 18th Street, as it has since the 1880s. It was designed by the most famous architect of the time, Henry Hobson Richardson, and built for $75,000. Richardson created for the Glessners an innovative house, a house to suit a city corner. The mansion is L-shaped around an inner courtyard. From the street, it looks like a fortress, but inside, the rooms turn their windows to a quiet, sunlit court.

The house was put to various uses after Glessner's death, but in 1966 it was up for sale. The lone survivor of four buildings Richardson had designed for Chicago, it stood empty and in sad need of repair. A young draftsman who worked for Mies van der Rohe's firm joined three friends to save the house. They formed a nonprofit organization, the Chicago School of Architecture Foundation, to raise money to buy and restore it.

The foundation has grown well beyond the original four members and has shortened its name to Chicago Architecture Foundation, but it is still headquartered at Glessner House. Restored to look as it did when the Glessners lived there, the house now is a museum, a city and national landmark, and a cornerstone of the Prairie Avenue Historic District. The Foundation offers public tours of the house, and also holds special events and other educational programs there.

26. LUDWIG MIES VAN DER ROHE   1886-1969

Mies came to this country from Nazi Germany in 1937. He became head of the school of architecture at Armour Institute (now the Illinois Institute of Technology) and also designed its campus. He formed his own architectural firm in 1940 and after his retirement from IIT in 1958 devoted himself wholly to his architectural practice.

The Federal Center in the Loop is one of the finest examples of his work. Mies is one of the most important of modern architects and certainly the most imitated. His simple steel and glass boxes are what he referred to as skin and bones construction. Bones of steel support the building; a skin of glass offers protection from the elements. In their direct expression of their underlying metal frame, Mies' buildings can be seen as the ultimate development of the principles of the Chicago School.

Originally regarded as a leader of the unadorned, geometric style of architecture known as the International Style, Mies spent his career perfecting his "universal" building. "Less is more," was his famous explanation. He felt it was the architect's role to reduce a building to a timeless, even anonymous structure. In this way, he felt, the building offered its users total freedom. They could put it to any function they chose, furnish it in any way they wished and change the interior space as their needs dictated.

Mies' grave marker reflects the same precision and simplicity that characterizes his architecture. The granite stone is black, like his buildings. It, too, should remain unchanged despite the effects of time, weather and pollution. The granite is not polished, but finely honed because that was the way Mies liked to finish stone. It was designed by Dirk Lohan, Mies' grandson and a member of his firm.

Before you leave this spot, don't forget to look across the lake at the Goodman mausoleum. From here, you get a good view of its lake entrance.

27. CYRUS HALL McCORMICK, JR.   1859-1936

As you cross the road and make your way to Marshall Field's monument, you pass through part of the McCormick plot. Here is the grave of Cyrus Hall McCormick, Jr., son of the inventor of the reaper. He was the first president of the International Harvester Company, formed in 1902 when the McCormick Harvesting Machine Company merged with competitors.

28. MARSHALL FIELD   1835-1906

Sculptor Daniel Chester French and architect Henry Bacon created this dignified memorial for Chicago's giant of commerce, Marshall Field. They are the same men who, a decade later in 1922, did the Lincoln Memorial in Washington, D.C. The sad-faced seated woman seems to foreshadow the Lincoln statue. French was one of the best-known sculptors of his time. He had been invited, along with Augustus Saint-Gaudens and Lorado Taft, other major sculptors of the period, to create works for the 1893 World's Fair.

French entitled the statue, *Memory*. Despite its air of melancholy, there is a strength and durability in the seated figure. Life on this earth must end, but as long as it has been a life of integrity, one may meet death with a calm courage, exemplified in the oak leaves the woman holds. How different from the chilling despair of Taft's *Eternal Silence.*

The symbol on the base — the staff with two serpents twined around it — is the caduceus, the staff of the Roman god Mercury. It's generally used as a symbol of the medical profession, but here it stands for commerce. Mercury was the god of commerce (not to mention manual skill, eloquence, cleverness, travel and thievery).

The sober Marshall Field was the city's most successful man of commerce. He was, in fact, its wealthiest citizen. At about the turn of the century, he was reputed to have a fortune of $75 million. He gave land to the University of Chicago and he left $8 million in his will to support and make permanent the Field Museum of Natural History, which he had built for the Fair.

Marshall Field's beginnings were humble enough. He had been a store clerk in his native Massachusetts before making his way to Chicago. He clerked in John Farwell's store here, becoming in a few years general manager and then a partner. In 1865, he and Levi Leiter, who was also with Farwell, established a retail store in partnership with Potter Palmer. A few years later, when Palmer left the business, it became Field, Leiter & Company. In 1881, Field bought out his partner and, from that time on, it was Marshall Field & Company. Field developed it into the largest wholesale and retail dry-goods enterprise in the world, with branches in several countries. Today, it remains as well-known a Chicago institution as the lakefront itself.

29. CYRUS McCORMICK   1809-84

A simple headstone marks the grave of a man whose name you probably learned in school: Cyrus McCormick, the inventor of the reaper.

He grew up in Virginia and followed in the footsteps of his father, an inventor of agricultural implements. Cyrus McCormick was only 22 when he created a machine that could cut many acres of wheat in a day. He spent the rest of his life improving upon his invention, fighting court battles to defend his patents against infringements and vigorously marketing his reaper across the country and the world.

In 1847, McCormick built a reaper factory on the north bank of the Chicago River. He became one of the city's largest employers and a millionaire. When that factory was destroyed by the Chicago Fire, he built another along the south branch of the river, at Blue Island and Western.

McCormick established an extensive network of agents who represented him throughout the farmlands. The agents sold the reaper, collected payments due (McCormick was a pioneer of installment buying), taught the farmer how to use the machine and made repairs on it as well.

During the Civil War, the McCormick reaper played an important role. Farmers used it to do the work of men who had gone to fight, and wheat production increased so greatly that the North had not only enough wheat to supply its needs but enough to sell abroad to pay for the war.

McCormick is buried here with his wife, Nettie, two of their children — Harold and Mary — and a grandchild, Fowler. (Harold was the husband of Edith Rockefeller, and Fowler was their son.)

The McCormicks' plot is a large, L-shaped one. It extends all the way to the road and to the left behind the Field plot.

Although there is a memorial to McCormick in Chicago — the Presbyterian theological seminary he supported generously was named for him after his death — there is none here in Graceland. Only land. But that in itself seems a fitting monument for the man who revolutionized farming.

30. RICHARD NICKEL   1928-72

Architectural photographer Richard Nickel met his untimely death in the ruins of Adler & Sullivan's Stock Exchange on LaSalle Street. When this noteworthy building was being demolished, despite public protest, to make way for a high-rise office building, Nickel got permission from the wrecking company to salvage as much of the ornament as he could. When he was missing for several days, his family and friends became worried. His car was found parked near the Loop, and it was feared that he had been hurt in the Stock Exchange rubble. The wrecking company stopped work and a search was made for Nickel among the ruins. His body was found May 9; he had been missing since April 13.

Nickel had been one of the first in the city to be concerned about architectural preservation. Now, the artifacts he collected and the photographs he took are about all we have left of a number of Adler & Sullivan buildings that once graced the Loop.

Nickel's friends purchased this spot at Graceland for him so that his grave would be near Louis Sullivan's. You can see Sullivan's monument from here, just behind the Kimball marker.

Chicago architects John Vinci and Lawrence Kenny designed the grave marker. Nickel had been working on a book on the work of Adler & Sullivan; Vinci and other friends of Nickel hope to complete it.

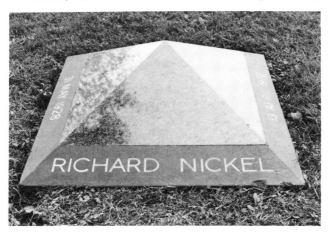

31. JOHN KRANZ   1841-1919

Kranz was a candy-maker. The Kranz Confectionery Store on State
Street was a favorite stop for shoppers from the time Kranz established
it in 1873 until it passed from the scene in the late 1940s.

32. MELVILLE FULLER   1833-1910

After receiving a law degree from Harvard, Fuller practiced law in
Chicago for many years and also served a term in the state legislature.
In 1888, President Cleveland appointed him Chief Justice of the
Supreme Court, a post he held for 22 years, until his death.

50

33. WILLIAM HULBERT   1832-82

This charming monument — a big baseball — marks the grave of the man who founded the National League of Professional Baseball Clubs. An ardent admirer of the game, Hulbert became involved in baseball in 1870 with the formation of the Chicago White Stockings. He was a stockholder in the club and became its president in 1875.

In 1876, Hulbert and Al Spalding, the White Stockings' new pitcher-manager, organized the National League with four teams from the West and four from the East. Their names are recorded on the stone baseball.

Hulbert served as league president from 1877 until his death. Early in his administration he expelled several players who had been found guilty of dishonesty and helped build confidence in the professional branch of baseball, which had been marked by gambling and corruption.

The White Stockings won the National League's first championship. Today, their descendants, the Chicago Cubs, play ball in Wrigley Field, not far from here.

34. WILLIAM M. HOYT   1837-1925

The towering monument gracing the plot of the Hoyt family is typical of Victorian cemetery art. In its display of emotion and its use of symbol, the statue is a good example of the lavish memorials the Victorians erected to express their grief. One of the three female figures of this statue bears a cross, representing faith and salvation; another holds an anchor, a symbol of hope; the third, nursing a child, embodies love and regeneration.

Vermonter William Hoyt made his way to Chicago in the 1850s, while still in his teens. He started out as a grocery clerk and ended up a prosperous wholesale grocer. Like so many others, he lost everything in the Chicago Fire of 1871. Like so many others, he immediately made a new start. He constructed a building on the site of the old Fort Dearborn and his company did business there until 1910.

The row of headstones to the right of the monument tells of an even greater loss Hoyt suffered by fire. You'll see that four of the headstones bear the same date of death: December 30, 1903. It's a date well-known in Chicago history.

On that day, fire broke out during a matinee performance at the Iroquois Theater. The frightened audience rushed to the exits. Those on the main floor managed to escape, but those in the balconies were trapped. Their bodies were found piled up behind locked fire doors and exits that opened inward. Six hundred people perished. Among them were Hoyt's daughter Emilie and her three children, aged 15, 12 and 9. Emilie's husband, Frederick Morton Fox, never recovered from the shock of the loss of his wife and children and he died a few months later.

35.   ALLAN PINKERTON   1819-84

A miniature obelisk marks the grave of the founder of the legendary Pinkerton Detective Agency. The plaque tells something of his career, but not the storybook beginnings.

When Allan Pinkerton came to this country from Scotland, he settled in Dundee, Ill., as a cooper, a maker of barrels. One day, while gathering wood on an island in the Fox River, he discovered the hideout of a gang of counterfeiters. He kept a discreet watch on the place and later aided the sheriff in capturing the lawbreakers.

For this and similar exploits, Pinkerton was offered the post of deputy sheriff of Kane County. When his reputation as a lawman spread, he

was appointed deputy sheriff of Cook County and then Chicago's first detective. He resigned from that job to form his private agency. As its trademark, he used the picture of an eye, unblinking and ever vigilant.

An ardent abolitionist, Pinkerton was part of the Underground Railway, helping escaped slaves make their way to Canada. When Abraham Lincoln received assassination threats before his inauguration as President, Pinkerton and his operatives saw to it that he arrived in Washington, D.C., unharmed. During the Civil War, Pinkerton established a secret service for Lincoln and served himself as a spy for the Union.

In 1869, Pinkerton suffered a paralyzing stroke. After that, he left the running of the agency to his two sons and turned to writing books about the work of the Pinkertons.

The agency became prominent across the country, but during the late 1800s, the Pinkertons came to be as much disliked by workingmen as by criminals. Factory owners like George Pullman and Cyrus McCormick employed the detectives to investigate union activity, prevent strikes and act as strikebreakers.

Next to the Pinkerton family plot is a plot for Pinkerton employees. Here you'll find the graves of Kate Warn, the first woman detective, and Timothy Webster. These two helped Pinkerton conduct Lincoln safely to his inauguration. Webster also served with Pinkerton's secret service during the Civil War. He was hanged by the Rebels when they discovered he was a Union spy. In the second row of headstones is a faded one for Joseph Whicher, who also died in the line of duty. He was killed while in pursuit of the Jesse James gang.

36. HOWARD VAN DOREN SHAW   1868-1926

Shaw was a contemporary of Frank Lloyd Wright and others of the Prairie School of Architecture, but he was not a part of the group. Wright and the Prairie School were bringing to residential architecture the same spirit of innovation that their forebears, the Chicago School, brought to commercial buildings. Shaw's designs remained traditional, drawing upon various styles of the past.

He designed his own home in Lake Forest, Ill., and spent a good part of his career building fine country homes for wealthy residents of that community and other North Shore suburbs. (He also did the William Goodman home in Chicago, in addition to the Goodman Theatre and the family's tomb, which we saw earlier.) His buildings were distinguished by fine workmanship and meticulous attention to detail.

These same qualities are apparent here. The Shaw family plot is bordered by plantings on three sides. The elegant polished granite pillar is surmounted by a bronze ball bearing the words of the 23rd Psalm. The twin red stones on either side of the plot at the front belong to two of Shaw's daughters and their husbands.

37. JOHN McCUTCHEON 1870-1949

McCutcheon married Howard Van Doren Shaw's daughter Evelyn in 1917. He had come to Chicago to work as a newspaper cartoonist after his graduation from Purdue University. He joined the *Tribune* in 1903 and was the paper's special cartoonist until his retirement in 1945. He was awarded a Pulitzer Prize in 1931. For many years, around Halloween, the *Trib* continued to print McCutcheon's cartoon, "Injun Summer," on its front page.

38. JOHN JONES 1816-79

Jones was a black man. That meant that in order to move to Illinois in the 1840s, he had to prove that he was a free man and not a slave. He had been born in North Carolina of a free mulatto woman and a German named Bromfield. His mother apprenticed him to a tailor so that he would have a trade.

Jones established a tailor shop in Chicago with only a few dollars to his name and built it into a successful enterprise. Since blacks were excluded from the schools, he taught himself to read and write. He aided fugitive slaves and fought to change the state's restrictive laws against blacks.

He became the first black man to hold elective office in Cook County. He was elected a county commissioner after the Fire and re-elected for a second term.

39. HENRY BROWN CLARKE   1801-1849

One of Chicago's first settlers, Clarke came west in 1835 from Utica, New York, seeking his fortune. He quickly succeeded in establishing himself as a partner in a wholesale hardware firm, and as a director of the small frontier town's first bank, the Illinois State Bank. But his success was shortlived. The expansive years of the early 1830s ended in the Panic of 1837, and almost overnight, Clarke's businesses failed. From that time until his death at 47 of cholera in 1849, Clarke supported his wife, Caroline, and their six children primarily by hunting and farming. Fifteen members of the Clarke family are buried in Graceland. Henry and Caroline were re-interred there in 1864; their stones are marked "FATHER" and "MOTHER."

The Clarkes are best remembered for the home they built. When they arrived in Chicago, they purchased land on the prairie a mile and a half south of town. In 1836, they built a fine Greek Revival house at about 17th and Michigan facing the lake. This solidly constructed house now is the oldest building in Chicago, having survived the Clarkes' change in fortune, the Chicago Fire of 1871, and a 28-block move south to 45th and Wabash. On a bitter winter day in 1977, the house again was uprooted as City engineers hauled it back "home" to the Prairie Avenue Historic District at 18th and Indiana, about a block from its original site.

The house has been restored to its original appearance and today is operated as a museum by the Chicago Architecture Foundation. A walk through this historic house allows visitors to vividly imagine the lives of Chicago's earliest families.

40. OUTDOOR MAUSOLEUM

Our final stop is the "high-rise" of graves just across the way from
Eternal Silence. It's quite unlike the mansions we have already seen.
There's no longer the space or the family fortunes to build lavish
memorials. A whole new crowd has moved in. Their cremated remains,
instead of being housed in grand monuments, are tucked away tidily in
little drawers. Times change, even in cemeteries.

BIBLIOGRAPHY

Andreas, A. T. *History of Chicago.* 3 vols. Chicago, 1885.

Banks, Nancy. "A City As Peaceful and Deserted As the Loop on Sunday," *Reader,* May 12, 1972.

Barnard, Harry. *Eagle Forgotten.* New York, 1938.

Blake, Peter. *Mies van der Rohe: Architecture and Structure.* Baltimore, 1960.

Bliss, Harry A. *Memorial Art, Ancient and Modern.* Buffalo, 1912.

Chicago Daily News. Robert Fitzsimmons' grave, Dec. 30, 1972, and April 24, 1973; Jack Johnson's grave, Nov. 4, 1969; Richard Nickel, May 10, 1972, Jan. 5, 1974, and April 13, 1974.

Chicago Sun-Times. Edith Rockefeller McCormick's burial, June 21, 1953; Richard Nickel's burial, May 12, 1972.

Chicago Tribune. Obituary of Frederick Morton Fox, March 3, 1904; William Goodman, March 23, 1936; William Hoyt, Dec. 18, 1925; William Hulbert, April 11, 1882; John Jones, May 22, 1879; Martin Ryerson, Sept. 7, 1887; Ossian Simonds, Nov. 22, 1931.

Condit, Carl. *The Chicago School of Architecture.* Chicago, 1964.

Connely, Willard. *Louis Sullivan As He Lived.* New York, 1960.

Corvey, Lane. "Birth of a Theatre: Goodman Theatre from 1925 to 1931." Master's thesis, Goodman Memorial Theatre and School of Drama, 1963.

"Crusader," *Art Digest,* VI (Oct. 1, 1931), 20.

Curl, James Stevens. *The Victorian Celebration of Death.* Detroit, 1972.

Dedmon, Emmett. *Fabulous Chicago.* New York, 1953.

Eaton, Leonard K. *Two Chicago Architects and Their Clients: Frank Lloyd Wright and Howard Van Doren Shaw.* Cambridge, Mass., 1969.

Gelbloom, Mara. "Ossian Simonds: Prairie Spirit in Landscape Gardening," *Prairie School Review,* XII (Second Quarter, 1975), 5-18.

Gilbert, Paul and Charles Lee Bryson. *Chicago and Its Makers.* Chicago, 1929.

Gordon, Charles Ulysses. Manuscript on history of Buena Park and Graceland. Chicago, 1950. (Chicago Historical Society Library)

Graceland Cemetery Office. "Catalogue of the Graceland Cemetery Lot Owners, to April, 1870." Chicago, 1870. (Chicago Historical Society Library)

Hoffman, Donald. *The Architecture of John Wellborn Root.* Baltimore, 1973.

Horan, James D. *The Pinkertons.* New York, 1967.

Leech, Harper and John Charles Carroll. *Armour and His Times.* New York, 1938.

Leonard, John W., ed. *The Book of Chicagoans.* Chicago, 1905.

Lewis, Lloyd and Henry Justin Smith. *Chicago, the History of Its Reputation.* New York, 1929.

"The Louis Sullivan Memorial," *Pencil Points,* IX (May, 1928), 305.

Mayer, Harold M. and Richard C. Wade. *Chicago: Growth of a Metropolis.* Chicago, 1969.

"Memorial to Louis Sullivan," *Western Architect,* XXXVIII (June, 1929), 100.

Miller, Nory. "A New Life for the Glessner House, that 'Granite Hut' on Prairie Avenue," *Inland Architect,* Sept., 1971. (Reprint available from Chicago School of Architecture Foundation)

"Monument to John Wellborn Root," *Inland Architect,* XXV (April, 1895), 27.

Moore, Charles. *The Life and Times of Charles Follen McKim.* New York, 1970.

Morley, John. *Death, Heaven and the Victorians.* Pittsburgh, 1971.

Morrison, Hugh. *Louis Sullivan, Prophet of Modern Architecture.* New York, 1935.

Newman, M. W. "Granite Hut," *Architectural Forum,* Nov., 1972. (Reprint available from Chicago School of Architecture Foundation)

New York Times. Victor Lawson obituary, Aug. 20, 1925.

Pierce, Bessie Louise. *A History of Chicago.* 3 vols. New York, 1957.

Poole, Ernest. *Giants Gone.* New York, 1943.

"The Proposition of the Graceland Cemetery Company and the Report thereon of the Committee of the Citizens of the Town of Lake View." Chicago, 1879. (Chicago Historial Society Library)

Randall, Frank A. *History of the Development of Building Construction in Chicago.* Urbana, 1949.

Tallmadge, Thomas Eddy. *Architecture in Old Chicago,* Chicago, 1941.

Tebbel, John. *American Dynasty: The Story of the McCormicks, Medills and Pattersons.* New York, 1947.

Wille, Lois. *Forever Open, Clear and Free.* Chicago, 1972.

▲
N

Graceland Cemetery

4001 NORTH CLARK STREET
CHICAGO, ILLINOIS 60613

1. Eli Williams
2. Dexter Graves
3. John Kinzie
4. Robert Fitzsimmons
5. Jack Johnson
6. Victor Lawson
7. John Root
8. Peter Schoenhofen
9. George Pullman
10. Martin Ryerson
11. Louis Sullivan
12. William Kimball
13. William Goodman
14. Potter Palmer
15. Charles Wacker
16. John Altgeld
17. Edith Rockefeller McCormick
18. Daniel Burnham
19. Ludwig Wolff
20. The Getty Tomb
21. Joseph Medill
22. Lambert Tree
23. Philip Armour
24. Lucius Fisher
25. John Glessner
26. Ludwig Mies van der Rohe
27. Cyrus Hall McCormick, Jr.
28. Marshall Field
29. Cyrus McCormick
30. Richard Nickel
31. John Kranz
32. Melville Fuller
33. William Hulbert
34. William M. Hoyt
35. Allan Pinkerton
36. Howard Van Doren Shaw
37. John McCutcheon
38. John Jones
39. Henry Brown Clarke
40. Outdoor Mausoleum